Publications International, Ltd.

Alcoa Consumer Products
Manager, Reynolds Kitchens: Betty T. Morton
Senior Home Economist: Patricia A. Schweitzer
Senior Home Economist: Charry E. Brown
Creative Development and Production Coordinator: Robin L. Irby

Pictured on the front cover: Pepper Steak Packets *(page 63).*

Pictured on the back cover (clockwise from top left): Spinach Lasagna *(page 17),* Mediterranean-Style Fish *(page 68),* Key Lime Bars *(page 21),* and Kansas City-Style Spareribs *(page 46).*

ISBN-13: 978-1-4127-2901-7
ISBN-10: 1-4127-2901-7

Manufactured in China.

8 7 6 5 4 3 2 1

Microwave Cooking: Microwave ovens vary in wattage. Use the cooking times as guidelines and check for doneness before adding more time.

Contents

53

58

32

79

From the Reynolds Kitchens to Yours...

Easy, delicious recipes to prolong that warm summer feeling all throughout the year.

By the time May rolls around, the promise of carefree summer meals beckons: enjoying dinner on the patio, spontaneous barbecue parties, picnics on the beach. The warmer months find families busier than ever, and the beautiful weather means no one wants to spend lots of time in the kitchen cooking and cleaning up. This time of year calls out for simple, delicious recipes that leave plenty of time to enjoy being outside and getting together with family and friends.

At the Reynolds Kitchens, all of our recipes, tips, and timesavers have been created to reflect the way we cook today. We have compiled more than 70 of our favorite summertime recipes in this cookbook, from tasty main dishes like Orange and Honey Glazed Chicken Breasts and Caribbean Shrimp Packets, to scrumptious side dishes like Grilled Marinated Vegetables, and mouthwatering desserts like Easy Grilled S'mores and Triple Chocolate Brownie Cake. You'll discover a variety of recipes that will simplify preparing food, whether you're cooking dinner for your family, grilling with the neighbors, or taking a dish to a Fourth of July picnic.

Most recipes feature our flagship brand, Reynolds Wrap® Aluminum Foil, but you will also find great recipe ideas using other Reynolds branded products like plastic wrap, parchment paper, foil and paper baking cups, oven bags, and slow cooker liners. No matter which of our products you use, you will enjoy quick, easy preparation, and easy cleanup.

Chipotle Barbecue Chicken
(page 42)

Reynolds Quick & Easy Packet Cooking

A simple, no mess way to make delicious homecooked meals.

When you wrap food in Reynolds Wrap® Heavy Duty Aluminum Foil packets and then oven bake or grill it, the ingredients cook evenly and quickly *and* there's no cleanup! Packet cooking also lets you customize your meals to suit the individual tastes in your family. If someone doesn't like an ingredient, such as pepper or onions, just leave that ingredient out of their foil packet. And for the family eating at different times, make up individual meals in foil packets and refrigerate. Packets can be baked in the oven one at a time or up to four at once as family schedules permit.

1. CENTER ingredients on a sheet (12×18 inches) of Reynolds Wrap Heavy Duty Aluminum Foil.

2. BRING up foil sides. Double fold top and ends to seal packet, leaving room for heat circulation inside. Repeat to make four packets.

3. BAKE on a cookie sheet in reheated 450°F oven, OR GRILL on medium-high in covered grill.

4. AFTER COOKING, open end of foil packet first to allow steam to escape. Then open top of foil packet.

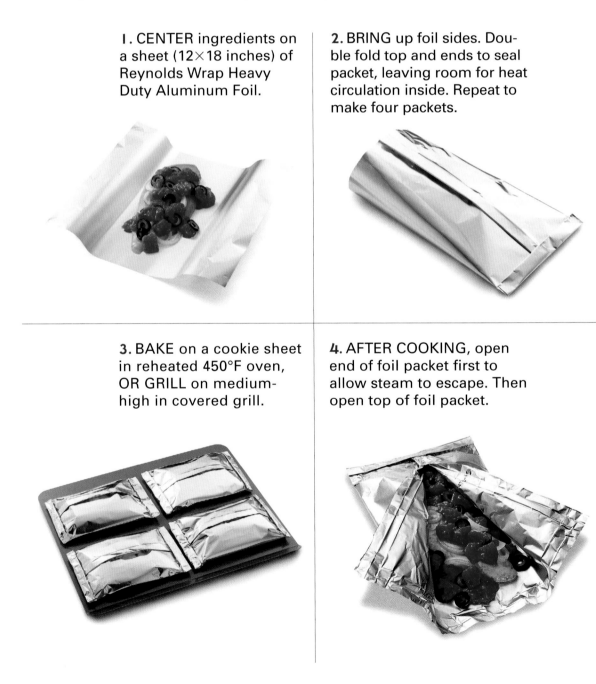

Packet Making Tip #1
Measure the Foil
When making a foil packet, use a 37½-square foot carton of Reynolds Wrap® Heavy Duty Aluminum Foil like a ruler to easily measure the foil sheet. Then tear the foil sheet off the roll. (50-square foot Heavy Duty Foil is 12 inches wide, and the 37½-square foot carton is 18 inches wide. You'll get a perfect 12×18-inch sheet for the packet.)

Packet Making Tip #2
Center the Food
Center the food on the foil sheet. This makes it easy to wrap the food to make the foil packet look neat.

Packet Making Tip #3
Layer the Food
Layer colorful vegetables on top of the chicken or fish to make an attractive presentation when the cooked foil packets are opened.

Packet Making Tip #4
Prevent Sticking
Use Reynolds Wrap® Release® Non-Stick Foil if working with ingredients like potatoes that may stick to the foil.

Packet Making Tip #5
How to Fold Foil Packets
For each foil packet, bring up the two sides of the foil and double fold with about 1-inch wide folds. Leave room for heat circulation inside the packet as the food cooks. Double fold each end to form the foil packet.

Packet Making Tip #6
Cooking Packets
Always place the foil packet(s) on a cookie sheet or in a shallow jelly roll pan. Four packets usually fit on a typical cookie sheet. The cookie sheet makes it easier to slide the packets in and out of the oven and it will catch any drips if the foil is accidentally torn.

Packet Making Tip #7
Handling Hot Packets
Be careful when removing the cooked foil packets from the cookie sheet. Use a pot holder or oven mitt to move the foil packet from the cookie sheet to a plate before opening.

Packet Making Tip #8
Open Carefully
After cooking, carefully open both ends of the foil packet first. Allow the hot steam to escape. Then open the top of the foil packet. Spoon the food from the packet onto the plate or serve the delicious, home-cooked food right from the foil packet.

Good to Go

Recipes that make it simple to take your meal on the road

Chunky Beef Vegetable Soup

Florentine Turkey Meat Loaf

Creamy Chicken Enchiladas

Spinach Lasagna

Al Fresco Garden Wrap

Prep Time: 10 minutes

	Reynolds® Plastic Wrap
1	(10- to 12-inch) flour tortilla **or** flat bread
2	large curly lettuce leaves
⅓	cup alfalfa sprouts
12	red, green and yellow bell pepper strips
¼	cup julienne cut carrots
4	cucumber slices, halved
4	grape tomatoes, sliced
2	tablespoons balsamic herb vinaigrette
1	tablespoon feta cheese

PULL out a 12-inch sheet of Reynolds Plastic Wrap; lay end of sheet on counter. Slide the EZ Slide Cutter to cut sheet.

PLACE tortilla on plastic wrap. Arrange lettuce leaves on tortilla. Top with alfalfa sprouts, pepper strips, carrots, cucumber and tomatoes. Drizzle with vinaigrette; sprinkle with feta cheese. Fold tortilla up over filling.

FOLD one end of plastic wrap up over bottom half of sandwich. Fold sides of plastic wrap tightly around sandwich, overlapping in back to seal. Overwrap whole sandwich if packing in a lunch box.

Makes 1 wrap sandwich

Reynolds Kitchens Tip

Reynolds Plastic Wrap with EZ Slide™ Cutter is great for wrapping sandwiches for lunch on-the-go. Reynolds Plastic Wrap seals tight and holds the sandwich together so it doesn't fall apart like a sandwich in a bag. For a party presentation with pizzazz, wrap the sandwiches in Reynolds Color Plastic Wrap and arrange them standing up in a clear bowl.

Overnight
BLT Salad

Summer Splash
Fruit Salad

Key Lime
Bars

Chocolate Chip
Toffee Bars

FunShapes Jell-O®
No Bake Mini
Cheesecakes

Chunky Beef Vegetable Soup

Prep Time: 15 minutes ■ **Cook Time:** 8 hours

1 Reynolds® Slow Cooker Liner

3 cups vegetable juice

2 cups hot water

1 pound beef for stew, cut into 1-inch cubes

8 cups frozen mixed vegetables

2 medium potatoes, peeled and cubed

1 small onion, chopped

¼ cup ketchup

3 tablespoons beef-flavor instant bouillon

½ teaspoon pepper

OPEN Reynolds Slow Cooker Liner and place it inside a 5- to 6½-quart slow cooker bowl. Fit liner snugly against the bottom and sides of bowl; pull top of liner over rim of bowl.

POUR the vegetable juice and water into the lined-slow cooker. Add beef, vegetables, ketchup, bouillon and pepper; stir gently. Place lid on slow cooker.

COOK on LOW for 8 to 9 hours **OR** on HIGH for 4 to 5 hours until beef is tender.

CAREFULLY remove lid to allow steam to escape. Serve food directly from lined slow cooker. Do not lift or transport liner with food inside. Cool slow cooker completely; remove liner and toss.

Makes 8 to 9 servings

Florentine Turkey Meat Loaf

Prep Time: 20 minutes ■ **Cook Time:** 1 hour

Reynolds Wrap® Release®
Non-Stick Foil

1¼ pounds ground turkey

1 cup spaghetti sauce, divided

½ cup Italian-seasoned bread crumbs

½ cup finely chopped onion

2 eggs (or 1 egg and 2 egg whites),
slightly beaten

2 tablespoons grated Parmesan
cheese

½ teaspoon fennel seed, crushed
(optional)

1 package (10 ounces) frozen chopped
spinach, thawed and well drained

¾ cup low-fat shredded mozzarella
cheese

PREHEAT oven to 350°F. Line an
8- or 9-inch loaf pan with Reynolds Wrap
Release Non-Stick Foil with non-stick (dull)
side toward food.

COMBINE ground turkey, ¼ cup spaghetti
sauce, bread crumbs, onion, eggs,
Parmesan cheese and fennel seed in
medium bowl.

PRESS half of turkey mixture into foil-lined
pan. Press a 1-inch indentation down center
of mixture, leaving 1-inch thickness on all
sides.

TOSS spinach and mozzarella cheese
together; spoon into indentation, mounding
in center. Press remaining turkey mixture
evenly over top, sealing edges.

BAKE 45 to 50 minutes. Spoon remaining
spaghetti sauce over meat loaf. Bake 15
minutes longer. Let stand 10 minutes.

Makes 6 to 8 servings

Creamy Chicken Enchiladas

Prep Time: 15 minutes ■ **Cook Time:** 25 minutes

Reynolds Wrap® Release®
Non-Stick Foil

2½ cups chopped cooked chicken

1 can (10¾ ounces) condensed cream
of chicken soup

1 cup Breakstone's® or Knudsen® Sour
Cream, divided

1½ cups Kraft® Shredded Colby &
Monterey Jack Cheese, divided

¼ cup chopped fresh cilantro, divided

12 Taco Bell® Home Originals® Flour
Tortillas

1½ cups Taco Bell® Home Originals®
Thick 'N Chunky Salsa

PREHEAT oven to 350°F. Line a 13×9×2-inch baking dish with Reynolds Wrap Release Non-Stick Foil with non-stick (dull) side toward food. Combine chicken, soup, ½ cup sour cream, ¾ cup cheese and 3 tablespoons cilantro.

SPOON about ¼ cup of the chicken mixture down center of each tortilla; roll up. Place, seam-sides down, in foil-lined baking dish; top with salsa and remaining ¾ cup cheese. Cover with foil, non-stick (dull) side down toward food.

BAKE 15 minutes; remove foil. Continue baking 10 minutes longer or until cheese is melted. Top with remaining cilantro and sour cream.

Makes 6 servings

Reynolds Kitchens Tip

Line pans with Release Non-Stick Foil before you cook to avoid scrubbing afterwards. Turn the pan upside down and press Release Non-Stick Foil (non-stick side down) around it. Remove the foil, flip the pan over and drop the foil inside. Crimp the edges and you're ready to cook!

No-Mess Barbecue Chicken

Prep Time: 5 minutes ■ **Cook Time:** 40 minutes

Reynolds Wrap® Release®
Non-Stick Foil

6 chicken pieces, skin removed
(1 chicken breast half, 2 thighs, 3
drumsticks)

⅔ cup barbecue sauce

PREHEAT oven to 450°F. Line a
13×9×2-inch pan with Reynolds Wrap
Release Non-Stick Foil with non-stick (dull)
side toward food.

BRUSH barbecue sauce over both sides of
chicken. Place chicken in foil-lined pan.
Reserve remaining barbecue sauce for
basting during baking.

BAKE 40 to 45 minutes, brushing top of
chicken with barbecue sauce every 15
minutes, until chicken is tender. Do not
brush with barbecue sauce during last 15
minutes of baking. Discard barbecue sauce.

Makes 4 to 6 servings

Reynolds Kitchens Tip

Try these flavors for variety.

Southwestern Barbecue Sauce: Add 2
teaspoons chili powder, 1 teaspoon dry
mustard, ¼ teaspoon garlic powder and
¼ teaspoon cayenne pepper to barbecue
sauce. Bake as directed above.

Tangy Sunshine Barbecue Sauce: Add 2
tablespoons orange juice concentrate to
barbecue sauce. Bake as directed above.

Vegetable Party Sub Sandwich

Prep Time: 20 minutes ■ **Chill Time:** 1 hour

Reynolds Wrap® Aluminum Foil
1 loaf unsliced French bread (1 pound loaf, 17×5 inches)
1 jar (4 ounces) chopped pimiento, drained
½ cup finely chopped celery
½ cup sliced green onion
⅔ cup mayonnaise or salad dressing
2 tablespoons Dijon-style mustard
1 teaspoon garlic salt
½ teaspoon pepper
3 cups bite-size pieces Romaine lettuce
1 ripe avocado, thinly sliced
1 large tomato, thinly sliced
¼ pound sliced Swiss cheese
1½ cups alfalfa sprouts
⅔ cup sliced ripe olives
1 cup shredded carrots
¼ pound sliced Cheddar cheese

TEAR off a sheet of Reynolds Wrap Aluminum Foil 2½ times the length of the bread. Slice bread in half lengthwise; place bottom half in center of foil sheet.

COMBINE pimiento, celery, onion, mayonnaise, mustard, garlic salt and pepper. Spread over cut sides of bread. Place 1½ cups lettuce on bottom half of bread.

LAYER half of avocado slices and half of tomato slices on bottom half of bread. Top with Swiss cheese, alfalfa sprouts, olives, carrots and cheddar cheese. Layer remaining tomato, avocado slices and 1½ cups lettuce on top of cheese. Place remaining half of bread on top.

BRING up foil sides. Double fold top and ends to seal packet. Refrigerate 1 to 2 hours before serving.

Makes 6 to 8 servings

Spinach Lasagna

Prep Time: 20 minutes ■ **Chill Time:** 1 hour

Reynolds Wrap® Release®
Non-Stick Foil

1	container (15 ounces) ricotta cheese
2	packages (10 ounces *each*) frozen chopped spinach, thawed, squeezed dry
1½	cups grated Parmesan cheese, divided
3	eggs
2	jars (28 ounces *each*) pasta sauce
12	lasagna noodles, cooked and drained
1	package (16 ounces) shredded mozzarella cheese

PREHEAT oven to 350°F.

COMBINE ricotta cheese, spinach, 1 cup Parmesan cheese and eggs in a large bowl; set aside.

SPREAD 1½ cups pasta sauce in pan. Arrange 3 lasagna noodles in a single layer on sauce; spoon 1½ cups ricotta mixture over noodles. Sprinkle with 1 cup mozzarella cheese.

REPEAT layering process two times. Arrange last 3 noodles over mozzarella cheese; spoon remaining sauce, mozzarella and Parmesan cheeses on top.

COVER with Reynolds Wrap Release Non-Stick Foil with non-stick (dull) side toward food.

BAKE 45 minutes. Remove foil and continue baking 15 minutes or until cheese is melted.

LET stand 15 minutes before serving.

Makes 10 to 12 servings

Overnight BLT Salad

Prep Time: 20 minutes ■ **Chill Time:** 4 hours

Reynolds® Plastic Wrap
1 cup (8 ounces) light ranch dressing
⅓ cup grated Parmesan cheese
¼ teaspoon freshly ground black pepper
4 cups torn Romaine lettuce
2 cups cubed cooked potatoes
1 medium tomato, chopped
1 package (10 ounces) frozen green peas, thawed
⅓ cup chopped green onions
4 slices turkey bacon, cooked and coarsely crumbled

COMBINE dressing, Parmesan cheese and pepper in a small bowl; set aside.

LAYER lettuce, potatoes, tomato and peas in a medium serving bowl. Spread with dressing mixture; sprinkle with green onions.

COVER with Reynolds Plastic Wrap; refrigerate at least 4 hours or overnight. Sprinkle with crumbled bacon before serving.

Makes 4 servings

Reynolds Kitchens Tips

For a colorful presentation, prepare the salad in a medium-size pedestal bowl and add a fluffy bow. To make a fluffy bow, tear off four 12-inch sheets of Reynolds Color Plastic Wrap. Pinch and twist the center of each sheet to make a small stem. Gather the four stems together like a bouquet of flowers; tie stems with a ribbon or a strip of plastic wrap. Gently fluff out ends of plastic wrap to make a bow; trim ends with scissors. Attach bow around foot of pedestal bowl with ribbon.

Make colorful ice bundles to keep your salad cool on a buffet table. For each ice bundle place 3 to 5 ice cubes on a 12-inch sheet of Reynolds Color Plastic Wrap. Bring up the corners of the plastic wrap and twist to hold ice cubes in the bundle. Place the salad bowl in the center of a large casserole dish or tray with sides. Arrange ice bundles on the tray around salad bowl and place on the buffet table.

Summer Splash Fruit Salad

Prep Time: 20 minutes ■ **Chill Time:** 30 minutes

Reynolds® Plastic Wrap
½ cup sweet orange marmalade
1 can (11 ounces) mandarin orange segments, drained, reserving ½ cup syrup
½ teaspoon almond extract
3 kiwi, peeled, thinly sliced
2 small peaches, cut in thin wedges
½ pint strawberries, halved
½ pint blueberries
1 cup seedless red or green grapes
1 cup *each*, cantaloupe and honeydew melon, cut in chunks

MIX orange marmalade, reserved syrup from mandarin oranges and almond extract in a small bowl; set aside.

COMBINE fruits in large glass serving bowl. Drizzle marmalade mixture over fruit.

COVER with Reynolds Plastic Wrap; refrigerate at least 30 minutes or until ready to serve.

Makes 8 to 10 servings

Reynolds Kitchens Tip

To make a layered fruit platter, arrange kiwi slices and mandarin orange segments just inside border of a 12-inch glass platter that is at least 1-inch deep. Arrange sliced peaches, strawberries and blueberries just inside the circle of kiwi and oranges to create the second layer. Arrange grapes to create the third layer. Mound the melons in the center of the grapes. Drizzle the marmalade mixture over all the fruit.

Key Lime Bars

Prep Time: 10 minutes ■ **Cook Time:** 35 minutes

Reynolds Wrap® Release®
Non-Stick Foil

CRUST

1½ cups flour

½ cup powdered sugar

¾ cup (1½) sticks butter, softened

FILLING

4 eggs

1½ cups granulated sugar

½ cup fresh key lime juice **OR** ¼ cup
lime juice plus ¼ cup lemon juice

2 tablespoons flour

2 to 3 teaspoons grated lime peel

PREHEAT oven to 350°F. Line a
13×9×2-inch baking pan with
Reynolds Wrap Release Non-Stick Foil
with non-stick (dull) side toward food.

COMBINE crust ingredients; press into foil-
lined pan.

BAKE 20 minutes; remove from oven.

COMBINE filling ingredients; spread over
baked crust.

RETURN to oven and **CONTINUE BAKING**
15 to 20 minutes or until filling is set and
bars are light brown around the edges. Cool
completely on a wire rack. Sprinkle with
additional powdered sugar. Use edges of
foil to lift bars from pan. Place on a cutting
board. Pull back edges of foil for easy
cutting.

Makes 24 bars

Reynolds Kitchens Tip

Line pans with Release Non-Stick Foil
before you cook to avoid scrubbing
afterwards. Turn the pan upside down and
press Release Non-Stick Foil (non-stick side
down) around it. Remove the foil, flip the
pan over and drop the foil inside. Crimp the
edges and you're ready to cook!

Chocolate Chip Toffee Bars

Prep Time: 12 minutes ■ **Cook Time:** 35 minutes

	Reynolds Wrap® Release® Non-Stick Foil
1	package (18 ounces) refrigerated chocolate chip cookie dough
1	can (14 ounces) sweetened condensed milk
1	cup almond toffee bits
1	cup sweetened flaked coconut, divided
½	cup sliced almonds, divided
1	cup semi-sweet chocolate chips

PREHEAT oven to 350°F. Line a 13×9×2-inch baking pan with Reynolds Wrap Release Non-Stick Foil with non-stick (dull) side toward food, extending foil over sides of pan.

PRESS cookie dough evenly into bottom of foil-lined pan.

BAKE 15 to 17 minutes or until lightly browned crust has formed on top of dough. Remove from oven.

COMBINE sweetened condensed milk, toffee bits, ½ cup coconut and ¼ cup almonds. Spread evenly over hot baked cookie dough. Sprinkle chocolate chips, remaining coconut and almonds over mixture. Return to oven.

CONTINUE BAKING 20 to 25 minutes until bubbly and coconut is a light golden brown. Cool in pan on a wire rack. Use foil to lift bars from pan onto a cutting board. Cut into bars.

Makes 36 bars

FunShapes Jell-O® No Bake Mini Cheesecakes

Prep Time: 15 minutes ■ **Chill Time:** 1 hour

12	Reynolds® FunShapes™ Stars or Hearts Baking Cups
1	package (11.1 ounces) Jell-O® No-Bake Real Cheesecake
2	tablespoons sugar
5	tablespoons butter or margarine, melted
1½	cups cold milk
	Fresh berries (optional)

PLACE Reynolds FunShapes Stars or Hearts Baking Cups on a cookie sheet with sides. Spray with nonstick cooking spray; set aside.

MIX Crust Mix, sugar and butter until well blended; set aside.

BEAT milk and Filling Mix with an electric mixer on low speed just until moistened. Beat on medium speed 3 minutes. (Filling will be thick.) Spoon about ¼ cup cheesecake mixture into each baking cup.

SPOON reserved crust mixture evenly over cheesecake mixture in baking cups.

REFRIGERATE at least 1 hour or until ready to serve. Invert cheesecakes onto serving plates. Remove baking cups. Store any leftover cheesecakes in refrigerator.

Makes 12 servings

Reynolds Kitchens Tip

Top with fresh berries just before serving.

Entertaining Made Easy

Easy preparation, presentation, and cleanup
means you can relax and enjoy the party

**Asparagus Bundles
with Prosciutto
& Goat Cheese**

**Apple Stuffed Pork
Chops**

**Chicken
en Papillote**

**Slow Cooker Asian
Pork Roast**

Pecan Coconut Crusted Fish with Pineapple Mango Salsa

Prep Time: 20 minutes ■ **Cook Time:** 15 minutes

Reynolds Wrap® Release®
Non-Stick Foil

¼ cup (½ stick) butter, melted

½ teaspoon salt

¼ to 1⁄2 teaspoon cayenne pepper

4 fish fillets (4 to 6 ounces *each*)

PECAN COATING

½ cup finely chopped pecans

½ cup sweetened, flaked coconut

2 tablespoons plain dry bread crumbs

PINEAPPLE MANGO SALSA

2 cans (8 ounces *each*) pineapple
tidbits, drained

1 large mango, peeled and diced

½ medium red bell pepper, diced

2 green onions, chopped

1 tablespoon red wine vinegar

2 tablespoons chopped fresh cilantro

¼ teaspoon salt

PREHEAT oven to 400°F. Line a 15×10×1-inch baking pan with Reynolds Wrap Release Non-Stick Foil with non-stick (dull) side toward food.

COMBINE butter, salt and cayenne pepper in a large bowl; add fish. Rub mixture on both sides of fish; set aside.

COMBINE pecans, coconut and bread crumbs on a sheet of Reynolds® Cut-Rite® Wax Paper. Roll fish in coconut mixture, turning to coat evenly. Place in a single layer in foil-lined pan. Place any remaining coconut mixture on top of fish.

BAKE 15 to 20 minutes or until fish flakes when tested with a fork.

FOR SALSA: While fish is baking, combine pineapple, mango, red pepper, green onions, red wine vinegar, cilantro and salt in a medium bowl. Cover with Reynolds® Plastic Wrap; refrigerate. Serve with fish.

Makes 4 servings

**Shrimp Cocktail
Stars**

**Baked Chile
Rellenos with
Roasted Corn**

**Herbed Vegetable
Packet**

**Triple Chocolate
Brownie Cake**

**Confetti
Party Pie**

Asparagus Bundles with Prosciutto & Goat Cheese

Prep Time: 8 minutes ■ **Cook Time:** 11 minutes

Reynolds Wrap® Heavy Duty Aluminum Foil

1 pound fresh asparagus, trimmed

2 thin slices prosciutto, cut in 1-inch wide strips

1 tablespoon olive oil

¼ teaspoon salt

⅛ teaspoon freshly ground black pepper

2 tablespoons chopped roasted red peppers

¼ cup crumbled goat or feta cheese

PREHEAT oven to 450°F. Line a 15×10×1-inch baking pan with Reynolds Wrap Heavy Duty Aluminum Foil.

WRAP asparagus spears in bundles of 3 or 4 around the middle with a strip of prosciutto. Place bundles in a single layer in foil-lined pan. Drizzle olive oil over asparagus bundles. Sprinkle with salt and pepper. Top with roasted red peppers.

BAKE 6 to 8 minutes or until asparagus is crisp-tender. Sprinkle with cheese.

CONTINUE BAKING 5 minutes longer or until cheese is softened and heated through.

Makes 6 servings

Two at Once Roasted Chickens

Prep Time: 10 minutes ■ **Cook Time:** 1¾ hours

1	Reynolds® Oven Bag, Turkey Size
1	tablespoon flour
2	medium onions, cut in eighths
4	stalks celery, sliced
2	whole roasting chickens (5 to 7 pounds each)
	Vegetable oil
	Salt and pepper

PREHEAT oven to 350°F.

SHAKE flour in Reynolds Oven Bag; place in a roasting pan at least 2 inches deep.

ADD vegetables to oven bag. Brush chickens with oil; sprinkle chickens with seasoned salt and pepper. Place chickens in oven bag on top of vegetables.

CLOSE oven bag with nylon tie; cut six ½-inch slits in top. Tuck ends of bag in pan.

BAKE 1¾ to 2 hours or until meat thermometer inserted in thickest part of thigh not touching the bone reads 180°F.

Makes 13 to 18 servings

Apple Stuffed Pork Chops

Prep Time: 15 minutes ■ **Cook Time:** 23 minutes

Reynolds Wrap® Heavy Duty
Aluminum Foil

4 boneless center cut pork chops (each about 1¼ inches thick), fat trimmed
1 package (6 ounces) stuffing mix for pork
½ cup chopped apple
¼ cup dried sweetened cranberries
½ teaspoon seasoned salt
¼ teaspoon pepper
2 tablespoons packed brown sugar
1 tablespoon butter, melted

PREHEAT oven to 425°F. Line a 15×10×1-inch pan with Reynolds Wrap Heavy Duty Aluminum Foil.

CUT a pocket in each pork chop with a sharp knife. Prepare stuffing mix following package directions. Stir in apple and cranberries.

PLACE chops in foil-lined pan; season with salt and pepper. Stuff each with ½ cup stuffing. Press to flatten.

BAKE 18 to 20 minutes. Remove from oven. Heat broiler. Mix brown sugar and butter; brush onto chops. Broil 3 to 4 inches from heat, 5 to 8 minutes or until brown.

Makes 4 servings

Chicken en Papillote

Prep Time: 15 minutes ■ **Cook Time:** 20 minutes

	Reynolds® Parchment Paper
¾	cup sun-dried tomatoes
4	boneless, skinless chicken breast halves (4 to 6 ounces *each*)
1	teaspoon dried basil or rosemary, crumbled
	Salt and pepper
1	medium zucchini or yellow squash, cut into julienne strips
1	cup sliced fresh mushrooms
4	teaspoons olive oil or butter

PREHEAT oven to 400°F.

TEAR off four 15-inch sheets of Reynolds Parchment Paper. Fold each parchment sheet in half and cut out a large heart shape, using folded edge as center of heart; set aside. Soak sun-dried tomatoes to rehydrate following package directions. Drain and set aside.

UNFOLD each parchment heart. Arrange one-fourth of sun-dried tomatoes on half of each heart near fold. Place one chicken breast half over tomatoes on each heart. Sprinkle chicken with basil, salt and pepper. Top with remaining vegetables and oil.

FOLD over other half of each heart to enclose ingredients. Starting at top of each heart, make small overlapping folds to seal edges together. Twist the last fold at the bottom of heart several times to make a tight seal; place parchment pouches on a large cookie sheet.

BAKE 20 to 25 minutes. Place parchment pouches on dinner plates. Carefully cut an "X" in top of each pouch to allow steam to escape.

Makes 4 servings

Slow Cooker Asian Pork Roast

Prep Time: 10 minutes ■ **Cook Time:** 5 hours

1	Reynolds® Slow Cooker Liner
	2-pound boneless pork loin roast
¾	cup salsa
½	cup honey roast flavored peanut butter
2	tablespoons soy sauce
2	tablespoons sesame oil
1	teaspoon fresh ginger, grated
¼ to ½	teaspoon cayenne pepper
3	cloves garlic, minced
	Hot cooked rice
¼	cup cashews **or** peanuts, coarsely chopped
2	tablespoons chopped green onion

OPEN Reynolds Slow Cooker Liner and place it inside a 5- to 6½-quart slow cooker bowl. Fit liner snugly against the bottom and sides of bowl; pull top of liner over rim of bowl.

PLACE pork roast in lined-slow cooker. Mix salsa, peanut butter, soy sauce, sesame oil, ginger, cayenne pepper and garlic in a medium bowl. Pour over roast. Place lid on slow cooker.

COOK on LOW for 5 to 6 hours or on HIGH for 3 to 4 hours or until meat thermometer inserted in roast reads 160°F.

CAREFULLY remove lid to allow steam to escape. Spoon rice onto a serving platter. Remove roast from slow cooker using slotted spoon and place on top of rice. Gently stir sauce with plastic or wooden spoon; spoon sauce over roast. Sprinkle with cashews and green onions. Do not lift or transport liner with food inside. Cool slow cooker completely; remove liner and discard.

Makes 8 (3 ounce) servings

Reynolds Kitchens Tip

After removing your food, just leave your slow cooker to cool while you enjoy your meal. When dinner is done, instead of soaking and scrubbing your slow cooker, just toss the liner and wipe the cooled slow cooker with a damp cloth or paper towel and put it away.

Honey Glazed Salmon

Prep Time: 10 minutes ■ **Cook Time:** 20 minutes

Reynolds Wrap® Release®
Non-Stick Foil

¼ cup honey

2 tablespoons Dijon-style mustard

1 tablespoon melted butter

1 teaspoon Worcestershire sauce

Salt and pepper

4 salmon fillets (4 to 6 ounces *each*)

1 pound fresh asparagus spears

½ cup chopped walnuts

PREHEAT oven to 400°F. Line a 13×9×2-inch baking pan with Reynolds Wrap Release Non-Stick Foil with non-stick (dull) side toward food. Combine honey, mustard, butter, Worcestershire sauce, salt and pepper; set aside.

PLACE salmon in center of foil-lined pan. Arrange asparagus around salmon. Sprinkle with walnuts; drizzle with reserved honey glaze.

BAKE 20 to 22 minutes or until salmon flakes easily when tested with a fork.

Makes 4 servings

Patio Party

Prep Time: 30 minutes ■ **Cook Time:** 12 minutes

12 Reynolds® FunShapes™ Stars or Hearts Baking Cups
Crabmeat Appetizers (recipe follows)
Shrimp Cocktail Stars (recipe follows)
No Double Dipping Salsa & Guacamole (recipe follows)

PREPARE Crabmeat Appetizers, Shrimp Cocktail Stars and No Double Dipping Salsa & Guacamole in Reynolds FunShapes Stars or Hearts Baking Cups.

ARRANGE FunShapes on platters and serve.

Makes 12 servings

Crabmeat Appetizers

Prep Time: 20 minutes ■ **Cook Time:** 12 minutes

12 Reynolds® FunShapes™ Stars Baking Cups
1 pound crabmeat
1 egg, beaten
⅓ cup mayonnaise
¼ cup finely chopped red bell pepper
2 tablespoons chopped fresh parsley
2 teaspoons seafood seasoning
1 teaspoon Worcestershire sauce
½ cup fresh bread crumbs
1 tablespoon butter, melted

PREHEAT oven to 400°F. Place Reynolds FunShapes Stars Baking Cups on a cookie sheet with sides; set aside.

COMBINE crabmeat, egg, mayonnaise, red pepper, parsley, seafood seasoning and Worcestershire sauce in a bowl until well blended.

SPOON about ¼ cup crabmeat mixture evenly into each baking cup.

COMBINE bread crumbs and butter in a small bowl. Sprinkle about ½ teaspoon over crabmeat mixture in each baking cup.

BAKE 12 to 14 minutes or until light brown.

Makes 12 servings

Crabmeat Appetizers

Shrimp Cocktail Stars

Prep Time: 10 minutes

12	Reynolds® FunShapes™ Stars Baking Cups
3	pounds cooked medium shrimp, peeled and deveined
	Cocktail sauce

PLACE Reynolds FunShapes Stars Baking Cups on a serving platter.

FILL each baking cup with desired amount of cocktail sauce. Place shrimp in the cocktail sauce, with the tails hanging over points of stars.

SERVE immediately or refrigerate until serving time.

Makes 12 servings

No Double Dipping Salsa & Guacamole

Prep Time: 5 minutes

12	Reynolds® FunShapes™ Stars or Hearts Baking Cups
	Your favorite salsa
	Your favorite guacamole

PLACE Reynolds FunShapes Stars or Hearts Baking Cups on a serving platter.

SPOON desired amount of salsa and guacamole into each baking cup. Serve immediately or refrigerate until serving time.

Makes 12 servings

Baked Chile Rellenos with Roasted Corn

Prep Time: 30 minutes ■ **Cook Time:** 15 minutes

Reynolds Wrap® Release® Non-Stick Aluminum Foil
8 poblano chiles
1 can (15¼ ounces) whole kernel corn, drained
5 tablespoons vegetable oil, divided
½ cup chopped roasted red pepper
½ cup chopped fresh cilantro
Salt and pepper to taste
2 cups grated Monterey Jack cheese
1 cup corn meal
½ cup dry bread crumbs
3 eggs
Your favorite tomato sauce or salsa

ROAST chiles under broiler, on the grill or over a flame until charred. Wrap in Reynolds® Plastic Wrap and let "sweat" about 10 minutes to loosen skin; peel. Carefully cut a slit down the side of each chile from just under the stem to ½ inch above the bottom pointed end. Scoop out all the seeds; set aside.

PREHEAT oven to 450°F. Line a 15×10×1-inch pan with Reynolds Wrap Release Non-Stick Foil with non-stick (dull) side toward food. Combine corn and 2 tablespoons oil. Spread in an even layer in foil-lined pan.

BAKE 20 to 25 minutes, stirring frequently until corn is roasted; let cool.

COMBINE roasted corn, red pepper, cilantro, salt and pepper. Stir in cheese. Stuff mixture into poblano chiles, overlapping the sides to enclose mixture.

LINE another 15×10×1-inch pan with Release Non-Stick Foil with non-stick (dull) side toward food.

MIX cornmeal, bread crumbs and remaining 3 tablespoons oil in a shallow bowl with a fork until well blended. Place eggs in another shallow bowl and beat lightly. Dip stuffed peppers in eggs, then in cornmeal mixture. Place in foil-lined pan.

BAKE 15 to 20 minutes or until golden brown. Serve with tomato sauce or salsa.

Makes 8 servings

Herbed Vegetable Packet

Prep Time: 12 minutes ■ **Cook Time:** 20 minutes

1 sheet (18×24 inches) Reynolds Wrap® Heavy Duty Aluminum Foil
3 cups broccoli florets
2 medium carrots, thinly sliced
1 medium yellow squash or zucchini, sliced
1 small onion, thinly sliced
1 teaspoon dried basil
1 teaspoon garlic salt
2 ice cubes
2 tablespoons butter or margarine

PREHEAT oven to 450°F **or** grill to medium-high.

CENTER vegetables on sheet of Reynolds Wrap Heavy Duty Aluminum Foil. Sprinkle with seasonings. Top with ice cubes and butter.

BRING up foil sides. Double fold top and ends to seal making one large foil packet, leaving room for heat circulation inside.

BAKE 20 to 25 minutes on a cookie sheet in oven **OR GRILL** 15 to 20 minutes in covered grill.

Makes: 4 to 6 servings

Grilled Sirloin with Salsa Criolla

Prep Time: 28 minutes ■ **Grill Time:** 16 minutes

Reynolds Wrap® Release®
Non-Stick Foil

1½-pound beef sirloin steak (about
1-inch thick), fat trimmed

SPICE RUB

1 teaspoon ground cumin

1 teaspoon dried oregano

1 teaspoon garlic powder

½ teaspoon salt

½ teaspoon coarsely ground black
pepper

SALSA

1 large tomato, seeded and diced

1 small green bell pepper, chopped

¼ cup finely chopped onion

¼ cup chopped cilantro

1 clove garlic, minced

2 tablespoons fresh lime juice

1 tablespoon vegetable oil

½ teaspoon ground cumin

¼ teaspoon salt

⅛ teaspoon coarsely ground black
pepper

PREHEAT grill to medium-high. Make drainage holes in sheet of Reynolds Wrap Release Non-Stick Foil with a large grilling fork; set aside. Combine Spice Rub ingredients. Rub mixture over both sides of steak. Cover with Reynolds® Plastic Wrap; let stand 15 minutes.

PLACE foil sheet with holes on grill grate with non-stick (dull) side toward food; immediately place steak on foil.

GRILL 7 to 9 minutes on each side or until meat thermometer reads 145°F for medium-rare or 160°F for medium.

FOR SALSA, combine all salsa ingredients in a medium bowl. Cover with plastic wrap; refrigerate until chilled. Serve with grilled steak.

Makes 4 servings

Triple Chocolate Brownie Cake

Prep Time: 20 minutes ■ **Cook Time:** 35 minutes

Reynolds® Parchment Paper

3 squares (1 ounce *each*) unsweetened chocolate, chopped

½ cup (1 stick) butter

3 eggs

1½ cups sugar

1 teaspoon vanilla extract

¼ teaspoon salt

1 cup flour

1 cup white chocolate chips

GLAZE

4 squares (1 ounce *each*) semi-sweet chocolate

3 tablespoons water

1½ tablespoons butter

2 teaspoons light corn syrup

PREHEAT oven to 350°F. Grease sides of a 9-inch round cake pan. Line bottom of cake pan with Reynolds Parchment Paper; set aside.

FOR CAKE, place unsweetened chocolate and butter in a microwave-safe bowl. Microwave on HIGH power 1 to 1½ minutes, stirring every 30 seconds, until melted. Cool; set aside. Beat eggs on medium speed with an electric mixer. Beat in sugar, vanilla and salt. Stir in melted chocolate, flour and white chocolate chips. Spread batter in parchment-lined pan.

BAKE 35 to 37 minutes. Cool in pan on rack 15 minutes. Loosen sides with a knife; invert cake onto plate. Peel off parchment. Cool. Cake will be dense and fudgy.

FOR GLAZE, place semi-sweet chocolate, water, butter and corn syrup in a microwave-safe bowl. Microwave on HIGH power 1 to 1½ minutes, stirring every 30 seconds, until melted. Cool. Slide parchment strips under cake edges. Spread glaze over cake. Remove parchment strips; refrigerate until glaze is set.

Makes 12 to 16 servings

Reynolds Kitchens Tip

The quickest way to line a cake pan is to place cake pan on a sheet of Reynolds Parchment Paper. Use a pencil to trace around bottom of pan. Cut out liner. Fit parchment liner in pan.

Confetti Party Pie

Prep Time: 20 minutes ■ **Cook Time:** 8 minutes ■ **Chill Time:** 3 hours

Reynolds® Plastic Wrap

CRUST

2¼ cups chocolate bear-shaped graham snacks, crushed

1 tablespoon sugar

⅓ cup butter or margarine, melted

FILLING

1 package (8 ounces) light cream cheese, softened

2 tablespoons sugar

1 carton (8 ounces) light frozen whipped topping, thawed

½ cup toffee or mini chocolate chips

TOPPINGS

3 tablespoons candy coated chocolate pieces

2 tablespoons colored sprinkles

PREHEAT oven to 375°F.

FOR CRUST, stir crumbs, 1 tablespoon sugar and butter until well blended. Press crumb mixture evenly into a 9-inch glass pie plate.

BAKE 8 minutes; cool on wire rack.

FOR FILLING, beat cream cheese and 2 tablespoons sugar, in a medium bowl, with an electric mixer until well blended. Fold in whipped topping and toffee chips. Pour into crust.

COVER with Reynolds Plastic Wrap and refrigerate 3 hours or overnight. Before serving, remove plastic wrap. Decorate with chocolate pieces and colored sprinkles.

Makes 10 to 12 servings

Simple Grilling

Even beginners can achieve professional
results with these fuss-free grilling recipes

Chipotle Barbecue
Chicken

Satay-Style
Beef

Garden
Vegetable Packet

North Carolina
Barbecue Pork

Lemon Herb Chicken Kabobs

Prep Time: 15 minutes ■ **Chill Time:** 30 minutes ■ **Grill Time:** 10 minutes

Reynolds Wrap® Release®
Non-Stick Foil

3 tablespoons fresh lemon juice

3 tablespoons olive oil, divided

1 tablespoon chopped fresh basil

1 clove garlic, minced

¼ teaspoon salt

¼ teaspoon freshly ground black
pepper

1 can (14 ounces) water packed
artichoke hearts, drained and
halved

1 pound boneless, skinless chicken
breast halves, cut into strips

16 broccoli florets

1 medium red bell pepper, cut into
1½-inch cubes

2 cups hot cooked rice (optional)

COMBINE lemon juice, 2 tablespoons olive oil, basil, garlic, salt and pepper in a large bowl. Add artichokes, chicken strips, broccoli and red pepper. Stir to coat ingredients with marinade.

COVER with Reynolds® Plastic Wrap; refrigerate 30 minutes to 1 hour. To prevent burning on grill, soak 8 bamboo skewers in water ½ hour before grilling.

PREHEAT grill to medium. Make drainage holes in a sheet of Reynolds Wrap Release Non-Stick Foil with a large grilling fork; set aside. For each kabob, alternately thread pieces of chicken and vegetables on skewers. Discard marinade. Brush kabobs with remaining 1 tablespoon olive oil.

PLACE foil sheet with holes on grill grate with non-stick (dull) side toward food; immediately place chicken kabobs on foil.

GRILL 5 to 6 minutes on each side or until chicken is tender. Serve over rice, if desired.

Makes 8 servings

**Grilled Marinated
Vegetables**

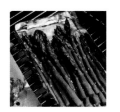

**Grilled
Asparagus**

**Sticky Louisiana
Barbecued Shrimp**

**Easy Grilled
S'mores**

**Savory
Grilled Pizzas**

Chipotle Barbecue Chicken

Prep Time: 10 minutes ■ **Grill Time:** 30 minutes

	Reynolds Wrap® Release® Non-Stick Foil
½	cup barbecue sauce
2	tablespoons packed dark brown sugar
2	tablespoons fresh lime juice
½ to 1	tablespoon chopped chipotle peppers in adobo sauce
6	chicken pieces

PREHEAT grill to medium. Make drainage holes in a sheet of Reynolds Wrap Release Non-Stick Foil with a large grilling fork; set aside. Combine barbecue sauce, brown sugar, lime juice and peppers; set aside.

PLACE foil sheet with holes on grill grate with non-stick (dull) side toward food; immediately place chicken, skin side up, on foil.

GRILL chicken 15 minutes in covered grill. Turn chicken; brush with half of sauce. Grill 10 minutes longer; turn chicken. Brush with remaining sauce; continue grilling 5 minutes or until chicken is tender and juices run clear or meat thermometer reads 170°F for breasts, 180°F for other pieces. Discard sauce.

REMOVE chicken from foil sheet. Serve immediately or cover with foil to keep warm until serving time.

Makes 4 servings

Reynolds Kitchens Tip

For drainage holes, lay a sheet of Release Non-Stick Foil over a cold grill grate, broiler pan or cooling rack. Make holes in the foil with a large grilling fork.

Texas-Heat Potato Packet

Prep Time: 15 minutes ■ **Grill Time:** 15 minutes

1 sheet (18×24 inches) Reynolds Wrap® Release® Non-Stick Foil

1⅓ pounds (4 medium) potatoes, cut in ½-inch cubes

2 tablespoons butter, cut into pieces

DRY RUB

2 teaspoons garlic powder

2 teaspoons paprika

2 teaspoons packed brown sugar

2 teaspoons salt

2 teaspoons black pepper

2 teaspoons cayenne pepper

PREHEAT grill to medium-high.

CENTER potatoes on sheet of Reynolds Wrap Release Non-Stick Foil with non-stick (dull) side toward food. Combine Dry Rub ingredients; sprinkle 2 teaspoons over potatoes. Top with butter. Reserve remaining Dry Rub for other uses.

BRING up foil sides. Double fold top and ends to form one large foil packet, leaving room for heat circulation inside.

GRILL 15 to 18 minutes in covered grill. Stir before serving.

Makes 4 servings

Reynolds Kitchens Tip

2 tablespoons olive oil can be substituted for the butter, if desired.

Satay-Style Beef

Prep Time: 25 minutes ■ **Grill Time:** 10 minutes

4 sheets (12×18 inches *each*)
   Reynolds Wrap® Heavy Duty
   Aluminum Foil

1 pound beef top sirloin steak,
   ½ inch thick, fat trimmed

3 cups fresh snow peas

⅓ cup reduced-sodium teriyaki sauce

2½ tablespoons creamy peanut butter

¾ teaspoon cornstarch

Angel hair pasta, cooked and
   drained

2 plum tomatoes, chopped

4 green onions, sliced

PREHEAT grill to medium-high. Slice steak across the grain into thin strips.

CENTER one-fourth of beef strips on each sheet of Reynolds Wrap Heavy Duty Aluminum Foil. Top with snow peas. Combine teriyaki sauce, peanut butter and cornstarch in a small bowl; mix until smooth and well blended. Pour teriyaki mixture evenly over meat and vegetables.

BRING up foil sides. Double fold top and ends to seal packet, leaving room for heat circulation inside. Repeat to make four packets.

GRILL 10 to 14 minutes in covered grill. Serve over angel hair pasta. Sprinkle each serving with tomatoes and green onions.

Makes 4 servings

Garden Vegetable Packet

Prep Time: 8 minutes ■ **Grill Time:** 15 minutes

1 sheet (18×24 inches)
  Reynolds Wrap® Heavy Duty
  Aluminum Foil

3 cups broccoli florets

2 cups cauliflower florets

½ medium red bell pepper, cut into
  1-inch pieces

1 teaspoon dried basil

½ teaspoon salt

⅛ teaspoon pepper

2 ice cubes

PREHEAT grill to medium-high.

CENTER broccoli, cauliflower and red pepper on sheet of Reynolds Wrap Heavy Duty Aluminum Foil. Sprinkle with basil, salt and pepper. Top with ice cubes.

BRING up foil sides. Double fold top and ends to seal making one large foil packet, leaving room for heat circulation inside.

GRILL 15 to 18 minutes in covered grill.

Makes 4 to 6 servings

Kansas City-Style Spareribs

Prep Time: 10 minutes ■ **Grill Time:** 1 hour

2 sheets (18×24 inches *each*)
Reynolds Wrap® Heavy Duty
Aluminum Foil

DRY RUB

¼ cup packed brown sugar

1 to 3 tablespoons salt

1 tablespoon chili powder

1 tablespoon black pepper

½ teaspoon ground allspice

½ teaspoon garlic powder

½ teaspoon onion powder

½ teaspoon celery salt

¼ teaspoon cayenne pepper

¼ teaspoon ground cumin

INGREDIENTS

3 pounds pork spareribs, cut in half

½ cup water

¾ cup barbecue sauce

PREHEAT grill to medium. Combine ingredients for Dry Rub in a small bowl; sprinkle over ribs and rub into meat, turning to coat ribs evenly.

CENTER half of ribs in single layer on each sheet of Reynolds Wrap Heavy Duty Aluminum Foil.

BRING up foil sides. Double fold top and one end. Through open end, add ½ cup water. Double fold remaining end to seal packet, leaving room for heat circulation inside. Repeat to make two packets.

GRILL 45 to 60 minutes in covered grill. Carefully remove ribs from foil; place ribs on grill and brush with barbecue sauce. **CONTINUE GRILLING** 10 to 15 minutes, brushing with sauce and turning every 5 minutes.

Makes 4 servings

North Carolina Barbecue Pork

Prep Time: 20 minutes ■ **Grill Time:** 2 hours

1	sheet (18×24 inches) Reynolds Wrap® Heavy Duty Aluminum Foil
3	pound boneless pork loin or shoulder roast

SPICE RUB

1	tablespoon sugar
1½	teaspoons salt
1½	teaspoons paprika
½	teaspoon pepper

VINEGAR-PEPPER SAUCE

1½	cups cider vinegar
2	tablespoons sugar
1	tablespoon crushed red pepper flakes
1½	teaspoons salt
¼	teaspoon cayenne pepper
1½	teaspoons Worcestershire sauce

SANDWICH SUGGESTION

Hamburger or sandwich buns

Cole slaw, hot pepper sauce (optional)

PREHEAT grill to medium.

COMBINE all Spice Rub ingredients. Sprinkle and rub seasoning over roast, turning to coat evenly. Center roast on sheet of Reynolds Wrap Heavy Duty Aluminum Foil. Combine all Vinegar-Pepper Sauce ingredients. Reserve ½ cup Vinegar-Pepper Sauce to use on sandwiches; set aside.

BRING up foil sides. Double fold one end to seal. Through open end, add ½ cup Vinegar-Pepper Sauce to packet; reserve remaining sauce for grilling roast. Double fold remaining end, leaving room for heat circulation inside packet.

GRILL 1½ hours or until roast is tender in covered grill. Carefully remove roast from foil and place directly on grill. Discard foil. Brush roast generously with remaining Vinegar-Pepper Sauce.

CONTINUE GRILLING 15 to 20 minutes on medium heat in uncovered grill, brushing with sauce and turning every 5 minutes to cook evenly. Remove roast from grill. Slice and shred roast while warm. Combine with reserved sauce. To make a sandwich, serve shredded pork on hamburger buns. Top with coleslaw and hot pepper sauce, if desired.

Makes 10 servings

Grilled Corn-on-the-Cob

Prep Time: 5 minutes ■ **Grill Time:** 15 minutes

1 sheet (18×24 inches) Reynolds Wrap® Heavy Duty Aluminum Foil

4 ears fresh corn-on-the-cob, husked

¼ cup butter or margarine, softened

Seasoned salt

Pepper

2 ice cubes

PREHEAT grill to medium-high.

CENTER corn on sheet of Reynolds Wrap Heavy Duty Aluminum Foil. Spread butter on corn. Sprinkle with seasonings. Top with ice cubes.

BRING up foil sides. Double fold top and ends to seal making one large foil packet, leaving room for heat circulation inside.

GRILL 15 to 20 minutes in covered grill, turning packet over once.

Makes 4 servings

Grilled Marinated Vegetables

Prep Time: 24 minutes ■ **Grill Time:** 8 minutes

Reynolds Wrap® Heavy Duty Aluminum Foil

1 small green bell pepper, cut into thin strips

1 small red or yellow bell pepper, cut into thin strips

1 small red onion, thinly sliced

1 package (8 ounces) fresh baby portobello mushrooms, halved

2 tablespoons chopped fresh basil or 1 tablespoon chopped fresh rosemary

3 tablespoons balsamic vinegar

2 tablespoons olive oil

2 cloves garlic, minced

Salt and black pepper to taste

PREHEAT grill to medium-high.

COMBINE vegetables, basil, vinegar, oil, garlic, salt and black pepper in a large bowl. Cover with Reynolds® Plastic Wrap and marinate at room temperature 15 to 20 minutes. Place vegetables in an even layer in a Reynolds Foil Do-It-Yourself (DIY) Grill Pan (to make a pan, see tip below). Slide pan onto grill grate.

GRILL 8 to 10 minutes in covered grill, turning frequently, until vegetables are crisp-tender. Slide foil pan from grill onto a cookie sheet to transport from the grill.

Makes 4 servings

Reynolds Kitchens Tip

To make a Reynolds Foil Do-It-Yourself (DIY) Grill Pan, stack two sheets of Release® Non-Stick Foil with non-stick (dull) side facing up. Flip a 13×9×2-inch pan upside down. Press sheets of foil around pan with non-stick (dull) side facing down. Remove foil from pan and crimp edges of foil to make a pan. Non-stick (dull) side should be facing up. Place DIY Grill Pan on a cookie sheet or tray to transport to and from the grill.

Ginger Sesame Salmon Packets

Prep Time: 10 minutes ■ **Grill Time:** 14 minutes

4 sheets (12×18 inches *each*) Reynolds Wrap® Release® Non-Stick Foil

4 thin onion slices, separated into rings

2 medium carrots, cut into julienne strips or shredded

4 salmon fillets (4 to 6 ounces *each*)

2 teaspoons grated fresh ginger

2 tablespoons seasoned rice vinegar

1 teaspoon sesame oil

Salt and pepper

Fresh spinach leaves

PREHEAT grill to medium-high.

CENTER one-fourth of onion slices and carrots on each sheet of Reynolds Wrap Release Non-Stick Foil with non-stick (dull) side toward food. Top with salmon. Sprinkle with ginger; drizzle with rice vinegar and sesame oil. Sprinkle with salt and pepper to taste.

BRING up foil sides. Double fold top and ends to seal packet, leaving room for heat circulation inside. Repeat to make four packets.

GRILL 14 to 18 minutes in covered grill. Serve salmon and vegetables on a bed of spinach. Sprinkle with additional seasoned rice vinegar, if desired.

Makes 4 servings

Grilled Asparagus

Prep Time: 5 minutes ■ **Grill Time:** 8 minutes

Reynolds Wrap® Release®
Non-Stick Foil

1 pound fresh asparagus, trimmed

2 tablespoons soy sauce

2 tablespoons butter, cut into small pieces

Freshly ground black pepper

1 tablespoon toasted sesame seeds (optional)

PREHEAT grill to medium-high.

ARRANGE asparagus in a single layer in a Reynolds Foil Do-It-Yourself (DIY) Grill Pan (to make a pan, see tip page 51). Drizzle with soy sauce. Dot with butter; sprinkle with pepper.

GRILL 8 to 10 minutes in covered grill or until tender, occasionally turning with tongs. Sprinkle with sesame seeds, if desired. Serve immediately.

Makes 4 servings

Sticky Louisiana Barbecued Shrimp

Prep Time: 18 minutes ■ **Chill Time:** 30 minutes ■ **Grill Time:** 4 minutes

	Reynolds Wrap® Release® Non-Stick Foil
¾	cup Worcestershire sauce
¼	cup plus 2 tablespoons barbecue sauce
1	tablespoon minced onion
2	cloves garlic, minced
2	teaspoons freshly ground black pepper
1	teaspoon salt
¼	teaspoon hot pepper sauce, or more to taste
1½	pounds large raw shrimp, peeled and deveined
2	tablespoons water
3	tablespoons butter, cut in chunks
2	tablespoons fresh lemon juice
	Hot cooked rice

COMBINE Worcestershire sauce, barbecue sauce, onion, garlic, pepper, salt and hot pepper sauce in a large bowl. Add shrimp; cover with Reynolds® Plastic Wrap. Marinate in refrigerator at least 30 minutes, stirring twice.

PREHEAT grill to high. Make drainage holes in a sheet of Reynolds Wrap Release Non-Stick Foil with a large grilling fork; set aside.

DRAIN marinade from shrimp into a medium saucepan. Rinse the bowl with the water and add to pan. Bring marinade to a boil and boil vigorously for 2 to 3 minutes. Add butter, stirring until melted. Remove from heat and stir in lemon juice. Reserve half of marinade for serving, cover with plastic wrap.

PLACE foil sheet with holes on grill grate with non-stick (dull) side toward food; immediately place shrimp in a single layer on foil. Brush with marinade.

GRILL 2 to 3 minutes; turn with tongs. Brush with remaining marinade. Discard marinade. **CONTINUE GRILLING** 2 to 3 minutes longer or until shrimp are firm with a few lightly browned edges. Serve immediately with additional sauce and rice.

Makes 4 servings

Easy Grilled S'mores

Prep Time: 5 minutes ■ **Grill Time:** 4 minutes

4	sheets (12×8 inches *each*) Reynolds Wrap® Heavy Duty Aluminum Foil
4	whole Honey Maid® honey graham crackers, broken crosswise in half (8 squares)
2	milk chocolate candy bars (1.55 ounces *each*), divided in half crosswise
4	Jet-Puffed® Marshmallows

PREHEAT grill to medium. For each S'more, top one graham cracker square with one candy bar half, one marshmallow and another graham cracker square. Repeat with remaining graham crackers, candy and marshmallows.

CENTER one S'more on each sheet of Reynolds Wrap Heavy Duty Aluminum Foil.

BRING up foil sides. Double fold top and ends to seal packet, leaving room for heat circulation inside. Repeat to make four packets.

GRILL 4 to 5 minutes in covered grill. Serve immediately.

Makes 4 servings

Savory Grilled Pizzas

Prep Time: 8 minutes ■ **Grill Time:** 8 minutes

1 sheet (12×18 inches)
Reynolds Wrap® Heavy Duty
Aluminum Foil

½ cup chunky salsa

2 (6-inch) Italian bread shells

¼ cup dry-roasted sunflower seeds

¼ cup ripe olives, cut into wedges

½ cup shredded Parmesan cheese

Fresh cilantro leaves

PREHEAT grill to medium.

SPOON salsa evenly onto bread shells. Sprinkle with sunflower seeds, olives and cheese.

PLACE sheet of Reynolds Wrap Heavy Duty Aluminum Foil on grill. Immediately place pizzas on foil.

GRILL 8 to 10 minutes in covered grill or until cheese is melted and pizzas are crispy. Slide foil sheet from grill onto a cookie sheet. Cut pizzas into wedges and garnish with cilantro.

Makes 2 servings

Light Suppers

Light and luscious and even easy enough to make for weeknight meals

Garden Vegetables and Pasta

Grilled Stuffed Peppers

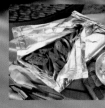

Pepper Steak Packets

Marinated Vegetable Salad

Dilled Fish with Vegetables

Prep Time: 10 minutes ■ **Cook Time:** 15 minutes

4 sheets (12×18 inches *each*)
Reynolds Wrap® Release®
Non-Stick Foil

1 lemon, thinly sliced

4 halibut or cod fillets (4 to 6 ounces *each*)

Salt and pepper

½ small zucchini, cut into thin strips

½ small yellow squash, cut into thin strips

1 medium carrot, cut into thin strips

1 medium onion, cut into thin wedges

1 teaspoon dried dill weed

PREHEAT oven to 450°F **OR** grill to medium-high.

CENTER several lemon slices on each sheet of Reynolds Wrap Release Non-Stick Foil with non-stick (dull) side toward food. Place fish on lemon slices. Sprinkle with salt and pepper. Top with zucchini, yellow squash, carrot and onion. Sprinkle dill weed over fish and vegetables.

BRING up foil sides. Double fold top and ends to seal packet, leaving room for heat circulation inside. Repeat to make four packets.

BAKE 15 to 18 minutes on a cookie sheet in oven **OR GRILL** 8 to 10 minutes in covered grill.

Makes 4 servings

**Mediterranean-
Style Fish**

**Southwestern
Chicken Salad**

**Turkey and
Wild Rice Salad**

**Tuscan Halibut
Packets**

**Sonoran Shrimp
with Chili Rice**

Garden Vegetables and Pasta

Prep Time: 15 minutes ■ **Cook Time:** 30 minutes

1 Reynolds® Oven Bag, Large Size
1 tablespoon flour
⅓ cup Italian dressing
2 cloves garlic, chopped
2 large tomatoes, cut into chunks
1 medium yellow squash, sliced
1 medium zucchini, sliced
Hot cooked pasta
Shredded Parmesan cheese

PREHEAT oven to 350°F.

SHAKE flour in Reynolds Oven Bag; place in a 13×9×2-inch or larger baking pan at least 2 inches deep.

ADD dressing and garlic to oven bag. Squeeze bag to blend in flour. Add tomatoes, yellow squash and zucchini to bag. Turn bag to coat vegetables with sauce. Arrange ingredients in an even layer in bag.

CLOSE oven bag with nylon tie; cut six ½-inch slits in top. Tuck ends of bag in pan.

BAKE 30 to 35 minutes until vegetables are crisp-tender. Serve over hot pasta. Sprinkle with Parmesan cheese.

Makes 4 servings

Reynolds Kitchens Tip

Substitute 3 tablespoons red wine vinegar, 2 tablespoons olive oil and 1 envelope (0.7 ounce) dry Italian dressing mix for the bottled Italian dressing, if desired.

Chicken with Apples and Almonds

Prep Time: 15 minutes ■ **Grill Time:** 12 minutes

4 sheets (12×18 inches *each*) Reynolds Wrap® Release® Non-Stick Foil

6 boneless, skinless chicken breast halves (4 to 6 ounces *each*)

Salt and pepper to taste

2 medium apples, each cored and cut into 8 wedges

½ cup packed brown sugar

¼ cup Dijon mustard

¼ cup sliced almonds

Ground cinnamon

PREHEAT grill to medium-high **OR** oven to 450°F. Sprinkle chicken with salt and pepper.

CENTER one chicken breast half on each sheet of Reynolds Wrap Release Non-Stick Foil with non-stick (dull) side toward food. Top chicken with apple wedges.

COMBINE brown sugar and mustard; spoon over apples and chicken. Sprinkle almonds and cinnamon on top.

BRING up foil sides. Double fold top and ends to seal packet, leaving room for heat circulation inside. Repeat to make four packets.

GRILL 12 to 14 minutes in covered grill **OR** **BAKE** 20 to 24 minutes on a cookie sheet in oven.

Makes 4 servings

Grilled Stuffed Peppers

Prep Time: 15 minutes ■ **Grill Time:** 10 minutes

2 sheets (18×20 inches *each*)
Reynolds Wrap® Release®
Non-Stick Foil

1 can (16 ounces) Great Northern
beans, rinsed and drained

½ cup stewed tomatoes, chopped

¾ teaspoon grated lemon peel

Salt and pepper to taste

2 large green bell peppers, halved
lengthwise (stem on, veins and
seeds removed)

PREHEAT grill to medium.

COMBINE beans, tomatoes, lemon peel,
salt and pepper; set aside.

ARRANGE pepper halves, cut-side down,
in a Reynolds Foil Do-It-Yourself (DIY) Grill
Pan (to make a pan, see tip page 51). Slide
pan onto grill grate.

GRILL 4 minutes in covered grill. Turn
peppers over, spoon about ½ cup bean
mixture into each pepper half. **CONTINUE
GRILLING** 6 to 8 minutes in covered grill
until filling is hot and peppers are tender.
Slide pan from grill onto cookie sheet to
transport from grill.

Makes 4 servings

Pepper Steak Packets

Prep Time: 10 minutes ■ **Cook Time:** 12 minutes

4 sheets (12×18 inches *each*) Reynolds Wrap® Heavy Duty Aluminum Foil

1 pound boneless beef sirloin steak, ½ inch thick, fat trimmed

½ teaspoon garlic powder

¼ teaspoon black pepper

1 medium green bell pepper, cut in strips

1 medium red bell pepper, cut in strips

½ cup teriyaki sauce

Hot cooked rice

PREHEAT oven to 450°F **OR** grill to medium-high. Cut steak into thin strips.

CENTER one-fourth of steak strips on each sheet of Reynolds Wrap Heavy Duty Aluminum Foil; sprinkle with garlic powder and black pepper. Top with bell pepper strips; drizzle with teriyaki sauce.

BRING up foil sides. Double fold top and ends to seal packet, leaving room for heat circulation inside. Repeat to make four packets.

BAKE 12 to 15 minutes on a cookie sheet in oven **OR GRILL** 7 to 9 minutes in covered grill. Serve over rice.

Makes 4 servings

Lemon Basil Chicken with Vegetables

Prep Time: 15 minutes ■ **Cook Time:** 1¼ hours

1 Reynolds® Oven Bag, Large Size
¼ cup flour
¼ cup fresh lemon juice
2 tablespoons each dried basil and rosemary, divided
2 teaspoons grated lemon peel, divided
½ teaspoon seasoned salt, divided
2 teaspoons paprika
2 small red potatoes, quartered
4 to 6 pound whole roasting chicken
1 small yellow squash, cut into large pieces
1 small zucchini, cut into large pieces
1 small red bell pepper, cut into 8 pieces

PREHEAT oven to 350°F.

SHAKE flour in Reynolds Oven Bag; place in a 13×9×2-inch or larger baking pan at least 2 inches deep. Add lemon juice, 1 tablespoon each basil and rosemary, 1 teaspoon lemon peel and ¼ teaspoon seasoned salt to bag. Squeeze bag to blend in flour.

ADD potatoes to oven bag. Turn bag to coat potatoes. Push potatoes to sides of bag. Combine remaining spices; spoon 2 teaspoons into chicken cavity. Sprinkle and rub remaining spices over entire chicken; place in center of bag with potatoes surrounding chicken. Arrange squash, zucchini and bell pepper over potatoes.

CLOSE oven bag with nylon tie; cut six ½-inch slits in top. Tuck ends of bag in pan.

BAKE 1¼ to 1½ hours or until meat thermometer inserted in thickest part of thigh not touching the bone reads 180°F. Let stand in oven bag 10 minutes; remove chicken from bag. Stir vegetables and sauce; serve over chicken.

Makes 5 to 6 servings

Reynolds Kitchens Tip

Substitute 4 large (about 1½ pounds) boneless, skinless chicken breast halves for the whole chicken. Bake 35 to 40 minutes or until meat thermometer reads 170°F. This shorter baking time will result in crisper vegetables than when baking the whole chicken.

Marinated Vegetable Salad

Prep Time: 10 minutes ■ **Cook Time:** 3 minutes ■ **Chill Time:** 4 hours

Reynolds® Plastic Wrap

3 cups broccoli florets

3 cups cauliflower florets

3 medium carrots, cut into julienne strips

2 tablespoons water

½ cup light Caesar dressing

½ cup roasted red pepper strips

¼ cup cubed red onion

PLACE broccoli, cauliflower and carrots in a 3-quart microwave-safe dish. Sprinkle with water. Cover dish with Reynolds Plastic Wrap, turning back one edge to vent.

MICROWAVE on HIGH power 3 to 4 minutes until vegetables are crisp-tender, stirring after 1½ minutes. Rinse with cold water; drain well. Place in a large serving bowl.

ADD dressing, red pepper strips and onion; stir to coat with dressing. Cover with plastic wrap. Refrigerate at least 4 hours or overnight.

Makes 6 servings

Greek Chicken Salad

Prep Time: 10 minutes ■ **Chill Time:** 2 hours

Reynolds® Plastic Wrap
2 cups cubed cooked chicken
1 can (15.8 ounces) Great Northern beans, rinsed and drained
1 can (2¼ ounces) sliced ripe olives, drained
12 cherry tomatoes, cut in half
1 medium cucumber, cut in half lengthwise and sliced
½ medium red onion, coarsely chopped
½ cup crumbled feta cheese
½ cup light Italian dressing
1 teaspoon dried oregano
Lettuce leaves

LAYER chicken, beans, olives, tomatoes, cucumber, onion and cheese in a medium bowl.

STIR together Italian dressing and oregano; pour over layered ingredients in bowl.

COVER with Reynolds Plastic Wrap; refrigerate for at least 2 hours or overnight. When ready to serve, gently toss and serve on lettuce leaves.

Makes 4 servings

Mediterranean-Style Fish

Prep Time: 15 minutes ■ **Cook Time:** 20 minutes

Reynolds Wrap® Heavy Duty Aluminum Foil

4 fresh fish fillets (4 to 6 ounces *each*)

2 cloves garlic, minced

½ teaspoon salt

¼ teaspoon pepper

1½ teaspoons herbes de Provence or dried salad herbs, divided

4 onion slices, separated into rings

1½ cups plum tomatoes, cut into 1-inch chunks

1 jar (6 ounces) marinated artichoke hearts, reserve 1 tablespoon marinade

¼ cup pitted Kalamata olives, halved

PREHEAT oven to 400°F. Line a 13×9×2-inch baking pan with Reynolds Wrap Heavy Duty Aluminum Foil.

ARRANGE fish fillets in pan. Rub garlic over top of fish. Sprinkle with salt, pepper and ¾ teaspoon herbes de Provence. Layer onion, tomatoes, artichoke hearts and olives over fish. Sprinkle with remaining herbes de Provence. Drizzle with reserved artichoke marinade.

BAKE 20 to 25 minutes or until fish flakes easily when tested with a fork. (If using frozen fish, bake 35 to 40 minutes.)

Makes 4 servings

Southwestern Chicken Salad

Prep Time: 15 minutes ■ **Microwave Time:** 3 minutes ■ **Chill Time:** 2 hours

Reynolds® Plastic Wrap

1 pound boneless, skinless chicken breast halves

3 to 4 teaspoons taco seasoning mix

3 tablespoons lime juice, divided

1 bunch Romaine lettuce, cut into strips

1 large red or green bell pepper, cubed

1 large ripe avocado, peeled and sliced

1 large tomato, cut into wedges

1 cup shredded Cheddar cheese

½ cup light sour cream

½ cup chunky salsa

CUT chicken breast halves into 1-inch cubes. Place chicken in an 8×8×2-inch microwave-safe baking dish; sprinkle with taco seasoning mix and toss to coat. Sprinkle with 1 tablespoon lime juice.

COVER dish with Reynolds Plastic Wrap, turning back one edge to vent. Stirring once after 2 minutes, microwave on HIGH 3 to 5 minutes or until chicken is tender.

ARRANGE romaine lettuce on large platter. Top with rows of chicken, red pepper, avocado slices, tomatoes and cheese. Sprinkle avocado slices with remaining lime juice to prevent darkening.

MIX sour cream and salsa. Garnish with chopped bell pepper, if desired.

COVER platter and dressing with plastic wrap; refrigerate at least 2 hours.

Makes 6 servings

Turkey Club Wrap Sandwich

Prep Time: 5 minutes

1	Reynolds® Wrappers™ Pop-Up Foil Sheet
1	(8-inch) flour tortilla
	Leafy lettuce
1	slice smoked turkey
1	slice ham
1	slice Swiss cheese
1	slice Cheddar cheese
	Mayonnaise
	Bacon bits
	Tomato slices

PLACE Reynolds Wrappers Pop-Up Foil Sheet on counter.

CENTER flour tortilla on foil sheet.

LAYER lettuce, turkey, ham and both cheeses on top of tortilla.

SPREAD with mayonnaise. Sprinkle with bacon bits. Top with tomato. Roll up tortilla.

WRAP filled tortilla, seam-side down in foil sheet.

Makes 1 serving

Turkey and Wild Rice Salad

Prep Time: 20 minutes ■ **Chill Time:** 1 hour

Reynolds® Plastic Wrap
3 cups cubed cooked turkey
2½ cups cooked wild rice
1 cup chopped carrots
¾ cup dried cherries or cranberries
½ cup sliced green onions
1 medium Granny Smith apple, cored and cubed
¼ cup orange juice
¼ cup apple cider vinegar
2 teaspoons Dijon-style mustard
½ cup vegetable oil
½ teaspoon salt
⅛ teaspoon pepper

COMBINE turkey, rice, carrots, cherries, green onions and apple in a large bowl.

BEAT orange juice, vinegar and mustard together in a small bowl. Slowly add oil, beating constantly. Stir in salt and pepper. Pour vinaigrette over turkey mixture; toss to blend.

COVER with Reynolds Plastic Wrap; refrigerate 1 to 2 hours until chilled.

Makes 4 to 6 servings

Reynolds Kitchens Tip

This recipe is a great way to use leftover turkey or chicken. For a shortcut, use turkey purchased from the supermarket deli.

Tuscan Halibut Packets

Prep Time: 10 minutes ■ **Cook Time:** 16 minutes

4 sheets (12×18 inches *each*) Reynolds Wrap® Heavy Duty Aluminum Foil

2 cans (15 ounces *each*) Great Northern or cannellini beans, rinsed, drained

2 medium tomatoes, chopped

1½ teaspoons dried basil, divided

4 halibut fillets (4 to 6 ounces *each*)

4 teaspoons olive oil

4 teaspoons lemon juice

2 teaspoons lemon pepper

4 lemon slices

PREHEAT oven to 450°F **OR** grill to medium-high. Combine beans, tomatoes, and ½ teaspoon basil.

CENTER one-fourth of bean mixture on each sheet of Reynolds Wrap Heavy Duty Aluminum Foil. Top with halibut; drizzle with olive oil and lemon juice. Sprinkle halibut with remaining basil and lemon pepper. Top with lemon slices.

BRING up foil sides. Double fold top and ends to seal packet, leaving room for heat circulation inside. Repeat to make four packets.

BAKE 16 to 20 minutes on a cookie sheet in oven **OR GRILL** 14 to 18 minutes in covered grill.

Makes 4 servings

Sonoran Shrimp with Chili Rice

Prep Time: 15 minutes ■ **Cook Time:** 14 minutes

4 sheets (12×18 inches *each*) Reynolds Wrap® Heavy Duty Aluminum Foil

1 package (10 ounces) frozen whole kernel corn, thawed

1 pound medium uncooked shrimp, peeled and deveined

1 cup salsa

4 teaspoons fresh lime juice

1 teaspoon roasted garlic oil or olive oil

CHILI RICE

2 cups instant brown rice

1 teaspoon chicken bouillon granules

1 teaspoon chili powder

PREHEAT oven to 450°F **OR** grill to medium-high.

CENTER one-fourth of corn on each sheet of Reynolds Wrap Heavy Duty Aluminum Foil. Top with shrimp and salsa. Drizzle with lime juice and oil.

BRING up foil sides. Double fold top and ends to seal packet, leaving room for heat circulation inside. Repeat to make four packets.

BAKE 14 to 18 minutes on a cookie sheet in oven **OR GRILL** 12 to 16 minutes in covered grill.

PREPARE chili rice while packets are cooking. Combine brown rice, chicken bouillon granules and chili powder; cook following brown rice package directions. Serve shrimp over chili rice.

Makes 4 servings

Grilled Jamaican-Style Chicken Salad

Prep Time: 15 minutes ■ **Chill Time:** 30 minutes ■ **Grill Time:** 10 minutes

Reynolds® Plastic Wrap

Reynolds Wrap® Release®
Non-Stick Foil

¾ cup oil and vinegar dressing

2 tablespoons Jamaican pepper sauce
or Caribbean-style steak sauce

1 teaspoon ground allspice

½ teaspoon dried thyme

4 green onions, sliced

4 boneless, skinless chicken breast
halves (4 to 6 ounces *each*)

1 package (10 ounces) salad mix or 8
cups torn lettuce

1 fresh mango, peeled and sliced

1 medium cucumber, sliced

¼ cup chopped cashews

COMBINE dressing, pepper sauce, allspice, thyme and green onions in a small bowl. Place chicken breasts in an 8×8×2-inch baking dish. Pour ½ of marinade over chicken; turn chicken to coat with marinade.

COVER with Reynolds Plastic Wrap; refrigerate at least 30 minutes. Cover remaining marinade with plastic wrap; refrigerate to use as dressing.

ARRANGE salad mix on four plates. Top with mango and cucumbers. Cover with plastic wrap: refrigerate until serving time.

PREHEAT grill to medium. Make drainage holes in a sheet of Reynolds Wrap Release Non-Stick Foil with a large grilling fork; set aside. Remove chicken from marinade. Discard marinade.

PLACE foil sheet with holes on grill grate with non-stick (dull) side toward food; immediately place chicken on foil.

GRILL 5 to 6 minutes on each side or until tender. Cut grilled chicken into strips. Place hot grilled chicken strips over salads. Drizzle with reserved marinade; sprinkle with cashews.

Makes 4 servings

Packet Cooking

Foil packets seal fresh flavors in and make cleanup a snap

Cajun Spiced Corn

Caribbean Shrimp Packets

Easy Pork Chop Packets

Fish Fillets Portobello

Tropical Chicken Packets

Prep Time: 8 minutes ■ **Cook Time:** 16 minutes

2 sheets (12×18 inches *each*) Reynolds Wrap® Heavy Duty Aluminum Foil

½ small onion, thinly sliced and separated into rings

2 boneless, skinless chicken breast halves (4 to 6 ounces *each*)

1 can (8 ounces) pineapple chunks, drained

½ medium red bell pepper, cut into strips

3 tablespoons teriyaki sauce

2 tablespoons packed brown sugar

½ teaspoon grated fresh ginger

2 cups hot cooked rice

PREHEAT oven to 450°F **OR** grill to medium-high.

CENTER onion slices on each sheet of Reynolds Wrap Heavy Duty Aluminum Foil. Top with chicken, pineapple and red pepper. Combine teriyaki sauce, brown sugar and ginger; spoon over chicken and vegetables.

BRING up foil sides. Double fold top and ends to seal packet, leaving room for heat circulation inside. Repeat to make two packets.

BAKE 16 to 18 minutes on a cookie sheet in oven **OR GRILL** 13 to 15 minutes in covered grill. Serve over rice with additional teriyaki sauce, if desired.

Makes 2 servings

Steak Topper Vegetable Packet

Pizzeria Chicken Packets

Salmon with Rainbow Peppers

Shrimp Creole Packets

Barbecue Sirloin Packet

Cajun Spiced Corn

Prep Time: 12 minutes ■ **Cook Time:** 20 minutes

1 sheet (18×24 inches)
Reynolds Wrap® Heavy Duty
Aluminum Foil

1 package (10 ounces) frozen whole
kernel corn

1 small onion, chopped

1 cup chopped tomatoes

¾ cup chopped green bell pepper

2 teaspoons Cajun seasoning

1 tablespoon butter or margarine

PREHEAT oven to 450°F **OR** grill to
medium-high.

CENTER vegetables on sheet of
Reynolds Wrap Heavy Duty Aluminum
Foil. Sprinkle with Cajun seasoning; stir
to blend. Top with butter.

BRING up foil sides. Double fold top and
ends to seal making one large foil packet,
leaving room for heat circulation inside.

BAKE 20 to 25 minutes on a cookie sheet
in oven **OR GRILL** 12 to 14 minutes in
covered grill.

Makes 4 servings

Reynolds Kitchens Tip

To make your own Cajun seasoning, combine 1½ teaspoons garlic powder, 1 teaspoon
salt, ¾ teaspoon dried basil, ¾ teaspoon dried thyme, ¾ teaspoon cayenne pepper, ½
teaspoon onion powder and ¼ teaspoon black pepper. Use 2 teaspoons mixture in above
recipe; reserve remaining mixture for another use.

Caribbean Shrimp Packets

Prep Time: 10 minutes ■ **Cook Time:** 12 minutes

4 sheets (12×18 inches *each*)
Reynolds Wrap® Heavy Duty
Aluminum Foil

1 can (15¼ ounces) pineapple chunks
in juice, drained

1½ pounds medium raw shrimp, peeled
and deveined

1 medium red bell pepper, chopped

1 medium jalapeno pepper, seeded
and finely chopped

1 tablespoon grated fresh ginger

1 tablespoon seafood seasoning

½ cup butter or margarine, cut into
pieces

¼ cup packed brown sugar

1½ tablespoons lemon juice

Hot cooked rice

PREHEAT oven to 450°F **OR** grill to
medium-high.

CENTER one fourth of pineapple chunks
on each sheet of Reynolds Wrap Heavy
Duty Aluminum Foil. Arrange shrimp in
even layer over pineapple. Combine
peppers, ginger and seasoning; sprinkle
over shrimp. Top with butter and brown
sugar. Drizzle with lemon juice.

BRING up foil sides. Double fold top and
ends to seal packet, leaving room for heat
circulation inside. Repeat to make four
packets.

BAKE 12 to 14 minutes on a cookie sheet
in oven **OR GRILL** 8 to 10 minutes in
covered grill. Serve over rice.

Makes 4 servings

Easy Pork Chop Packets

Prep Time: 10 minutes ■ **Cook Time:** 16 minutes

4 sheets (12×18 inches *each*) Reynolds Wrap® Heavy Duty Aluminum Foil

1 small onion, thinly sliced

4 boneless pork chops, about ½ inch thick

Salt and pepper to taste

1 can (10¾ ounces) condensed cream of mushroom soup, undiluted

2 tablespoons soy sauce

1 medium green bell pepper, sliced

Hot cooked rice

PREHEAT oven to 450°F **OR** grill to medium-high.

CENTER onion slices on each sheet of Reynolds Wrap Heavy Duty Aluminum Foil. Top with pork chops; sprinkle with salt and pepper. Combine cream of mushroom soup and soy sauce; spoon over pork chops. Top with green pepper slices.

BRING up foil sides. Double fold top and ends to seal packet, leaving room for heat circulation inside. Repeat to make four packets.

BAKE 16 to 18 minutes on a cookie sheet in oven **OR GRILL** 10 to 12 minutes in covered grill. Serve over rice.

Makes 4 servings

Herbed Fish and Vegetable Packet

Prep Time: 8 minutes ■ **Cook Time:** 18 minutes

4 sheets (12×18 inches *each*) Reynolds Wrap® Heavy Duty Aluminum Foil

4 fish fillets (4 to 6 ounces *each*)

½ teaspoon dried thyme

½ teaspoon dried marjoram

4 teaspoons fresh lemon juice

1 package (16 ounces) frozen broccoli, carrots and cauliflower

¼ cup chopped green onions

Salt and pepper to taste

2 tablespoons butter or margarine, cut in pieces

PREHEAT oven to 450°F **OR** grill to medium-high.

CENTER one fish fillet on each sheet of Reynolds Wrap Heavy Duty Aluminum Foil. Sprinkle fish with thyme, marjoram and lemon juice. Place frozen vegetables next to fish on each foil sheet. Sprinkle fish and vegetables with green onions, salt and pepper. Top with butter.

BRING up foil sides. Double fold top and ends to seal packet, leaving room for heat circulation inside. Repeat to make four packets.

BAKE 18 to 22 minutes on a cookie sheet in oven **OR GRILL** 16 to 20 minutes in covered grill.

Makes 4 servings

Chicken with Pine Nut Couscous

Prep Time: 10 minutes ■ **Cook Time:** 22 minutes

2 sheets (12×18 inches *each*) Reynolds Wrap® Release® Non-Stick Aluminum Foil

2 boneless, skinless chicken breast halves (4 to 6 ounces *each*)

1 package (5.6 ounces) pine nut couscous mix

2 tablespoons olive oil

1 medium zucchini, sliced

1 cup cherry tomatoes

½ teaspoon dried basil

8 ice cubes

⅔ cup water

PREHEAT oven to 450°F **OR** grill to medium-high.

CENTER one chicken breast half on each sheet of Reynolds Wrap Release Non-Stick Foil with the non-stick (dull) side toward food. Arrange couscous around each chicken breast. Sprinkle chicken and couscous with spices from mix; drizzle with olive oil. Top with zucchini and tomatoes; sprinkle with basil. Place ice cubes on couscous.

BRING up foil sides. Double fold top and one end of each packet. Through open end, pour ⅓ cup water into each packet. Double fold remaining end to seal packets, leaving room for heat circulation inside. Repeat to make two packets.

BAKE 22 to 24 minutes on a cookie sheet in oven **OR GRILL** 12 to 14 minutes in covered grill.

Makes 2 servings

Reynolds Kitchens Tip

To pour liquids into packets, hold packets at a slight angle. After folding ends to seal, turn folded ends up to prevent leaking.

Grilled Bean and Rice Burritos

Prep Time: 15 minutes ■ **Grill Time:** 12 minutes

4 sheets (12×18 inches *each*) Reynolds Wrap® Heavy Duty Aluminum Foil

1 can (16 ounces) refried beans

1⅓ cups cooked rice

1⅓ cups shredded Cheddar cheese

1⅓ cups chunky salsa

½ cup chopped green onion

2 tablespoons chopped fresh cilantro

4 (10- to 12-inch) flour tortillas

PREHEAT grill to medium-high **OR** oven to 450°F. Combine beans, rice, cheese, salsa, onion and cilantro in a medium bowl; set aside. Microwave tortillas on HIGH power 15 to 20 seconds until soft.

CENTER one tortilla on each sheet of Reynolds Wrap Heavy Duty Aluminum Foil. Spoon one-fourth of bean mixture in center of each tortilla. Wrap filling in each tortilla burrito-style. Center burrito on foil sheet seam-side down.

BRING up foil sides. Double fold top and ends to seal packet, leaving room for heat circulation inside. Repeat to make four packets.

GRILL 12 to 16 minutes in covered grill, turning once half way through grilling **OR** **BAKE** 18 to 20 minutes on a cookie sheet in oven.

Makes 4 servings

Baby Back Barbecue Ribs

Prep Time: 5 minutes ■ **Grill Time:** 1 hour

2 sheets (18×24 inches *each*) Reynolds Wrap® Heavy Duty Aluminum Foil

3 pounds baby back pork ribs

1 tablespoon packed brown sugar

1 tablespoon paprika

2 teaspoons garlic powder

1½ teaspoons pepper

½ cup water

1½ cups barbecue sauce

PREHEAT grill to medium.

CENTER half of ribs on each sheet of Reynolds Wrap Heavy Duty Aluminum Foil.

Combine brown sugar and spices; rub over ribs, turning to coat evenly.

BRING up foil sides. Double fold top and one end to seal packet. Through open end, add ¼ cup of water or 3 to 4 ice cubes. Double fold remaining end, leaving room for heat circulation inside. Repeat to make two packets.

GRILL for 45 to 60 minutes in covered grill. Remove ribs from foil; place ribs on grill.

BRUSH ribs with barbecue sauce. **CONTINUE GRILLING** 10 to 15 minutes, brushing with sauce and turning every 5 minutes.

Makes: 5 servings

Fish Fillets Portobello

Prep Time: 10 minutes ■ **Cook Time:** 20 minutes

4 sheets (12×18 inches *each*) Reynolds Wrap® Heavy Duty Aluminum Foil

4 fish fillets (4 to 6 ounces *each*)

1 tablespoon anchovy paste

1½ cups seeded and diced fresh tomatoes or 1 can (14½ ounces) diced tomatoes in juice, drained

1 can (2½ ounces) sliced black olives, drained

⅓ cup finely chopped onion

2 tablespoons capers, drained

1 teaspoon minced garlic

2 fresh portobello mushrooms

PREHEAT oven to 450°F **OR** grill to medium-high.

CENTER one fish fillet on each sheet of Reynolds Wrap Heavy Duty Aluminum Foil. Spread anchovy paste over top of fish. Combine tomatoes, olives, onion, capers and garlic; set aside. Cut four thin slices off one mushroom; set slices aside. Chop remaining mushrooms and combine with vegetables. Spoon one-fourth of vegetables over fish. Top each with one mushroom slice.

BRING up foil sides. Double fold top and ends to seal packet, leaving room for heat circulation inside. Repeat to make four packets.

BAKE 20 to 24 minutes on a cookie sheet in oven **OR GRILL** 9 to 11 minutes in covered grill.

Makes 4 servings

Italian Chicken & Veggies

Prep Time: 8 minutes ■ **Cook Time:** 20 minutes

4 sheets (12×18 inches *each*) Reynolds Wrap® Heavy Duty Aluminum Foil

4 boneless, skinless chicken breast halves (4 to 6 ounces *each*)

1⅓ cups fat-free Italian dressing

2 teaspoons dried basil

4 cups frozen broccoli, cauliflower and carrots

¼ cup grated Parmesan cheese

PREHEAT oven to 450°F **OR** grill to medium-high.

CENTER one chicken breast half on each sheet of Reynolds Wrap Heavy Duty Aluminum Foil. Pour Italian dressing over chicken; sprinkle with basil. Arrange vegetables on top of chicken.

BRING up foil sides. Double fold top and ends to seal packet, leaving room for heat circulation inside. Repeat to make four packets.

BAKE 20 to 22 minutes on a cookie sheet in oven **OR GRILL** 12 to 14 minutes in covered grill. Sprinkle with Parmesan cheese.

Makes 4 servings

SERVING SUGGESTION:
Serve over hot cooked pasta.

Steak Topper Vegetable Packet

Prep Time: 18 minutes ■ **Grill Time:** 15 minutes

1 sheet (18×24 inches) Reynolds Wrap® Heavy Duty Aluminum Foil

4 red onion slices

1 medium red bell pepper, cut into thin strips

1 medium yellow bell pepper, cut into thin strips

1 package (8 ounces) fresh baby portobello mushrooms, halved

2 cloves garlic, minced

2 tablespoons chopped fresh basil

1 tablespoon balsamic vinegar

1 tablespoon olive oil

Salt and pepper to taste

PREHEAT grill to medium-high **OR** oven to 450°F.

CENTER onion slices on sheet of Reynolds Wrap Heavy Duty Aluminum Foil. Combine peppers, mushrooms, garlic, basil, vinegar, olive oil, salt and pepper in a large bowl. Arrange vegetable mixture over onion slices in an even layer.

BRING up foil sides. Double fold top and ends to seal making one large foil packet, leaving room for heat circulation inside.

GRILL 15 to 20 minutes in covered grill **OR BAKE** 20 to 25 minutes on a cookie sheet in oven.

Makes 4 servings

Hot & Spicy Beef with Vegetables

Prep Time: 10 minutes ■ **Cook Time:** 18 minutes

2 sheets (12×18 inches *each*)
Reynolds Wrap® Release®
Non-Stick Foil

½ pound boneless beef sirloin steak,
fat trimmed, cubed

1½ teaspoons Mexican seasoning blend,
divided

1 medium zucchini, sliced ¼ inch thick

1 medium red bell pepper, sliced into
thin strips

1 can (8¾ ounces) whole kernel corn,
drained

⅓ cup beef gravy

½ teaspoon salt

Hot cooked rice (optional)

PREHEAT oven to 450°F **OR** grill to medium-high.

CENTER one-half of steak cubes on each sheet of Reynolds Wrap Release Non-Stick Foil with non-stick (dull) side toward food; sprinkle with ½ teaspoon Mexican seasoning. Arrange zucchini, red pepper and corn on top of steak. Combine gravy, remaining Mexican seasoning and salt; drizzle over beef and vegetables.

BRING up foil sides. Double fold top and ends to seal packet, leaving room for heat circulation inside. Repeat to make two packets.

BAKE 18 to 20 minutes on a cookie sheet in oven **OR GRILL** 10 to 12 minutes in covered grill. Serve hot over cooked rice, if desired.

Makes 2 servings

Pizzeria Chicken Packets

Prep Time: 20 minutes ■ **Cook Time:** 20 minutes

4 sheets (12×18 inches *each*)
Reynolds Wrap® Release®
Non-Stick Foil

4 boneless, skinless chicken breast
halves (4 to 6 ounces *each*)

1 cup pizza or spaghetti sauce

1 cup shredded low-fat mozzarella
cheese

20 slices pepperoni

1 medium green bell pepper, chopped

1 small onion, chopped

PREHEAT oven to 450°F **OR** grill to medium-high.

CENTER one chicken breast half on each sheet of Reynolds Wrap Release Non-Stick Foil with non-stick (dull) side toward food. Spoon pizza sauce over chicken. Sprinkle with cheese; top with pepperoni, green pepper and onion.

BRING up foil sides. Double fold top and ends to seal packet, leaving room for heat circulation inside. Repeat to make four packets.

BAKE 20 to 24 minutes on a cookie sheet in oven **OR GRILL** 12 to 14 minutes in covered grill or until chicken is tender and juices run clear or meat thermometer reads 170°F.

Makes 4 servings

Salmon with Rainbow Peppers

Prep Time: 10 minutes ■ **Cook Time:** 18 minutes

4 sheets (12×18 inches *each*) Reynolds Wrap® Heavy Duty Aluminum Foil

4 salmon fillets (4 to 6 ounces *each*)

4 medium red, yellow or green bell peppers, cut into strips

¼ cup butter or margarine, cut into pieces

1½ teaspoons dried basil

PREHEAT oven to 450°F **OR** grill to medium-high.

CENTER one salmon fillet on each sheet of Reynolds Wrap Heavy Duty Aluminum Foil. Arrange pepper strips around salmon. Top with butter and sprinkle with basil.

BRING up foil sides. Double fold top and ends to seal packet, leaving room for heat circulation inside. Repeat to make four packets.

BAKE 18 to 20 minutes on a cookie sheet in oven **OR GRILL** 16 to 18 minutes in covered grill.

Makes 4 servings

Shrimp Creole Packets

Prep Time: 10 minutes ■ **Cook Time:** 14 minutes

4 sheets (12×18 inches *each*)
  Reynolds Wrap® Release®
  Non-Stick Foil

3 cups cooked rice

1 can (14½ ounces) diced tomatoes
  with garlic and onion

1 medium green bell pepper, chopped

½ cup sliced celery

½ cup chopped onion

1 tablespoon Creole seasoning

2 to 3 teaspoons packed brown sugar

½ teaspoon dried oregano

1 pound medium raw shrimp, peeled
  and deveined

PREHEAT oven to 450°F **OR** grill to medium-high. Combine rice, tomatoes, green pepper, celery, onion, Creole seasoning, brown sugar and oregano. Stir in shrimp.

CENTER one-fourth of mixture on each sheet of Reynolds Wrap Release Non-Stick Foil with non-stick (dull) side toward food.

BRING up foil sides. Double fold top and ends to seal packet, leaving room for heat circulation inside. Repeat to make four packets.

BAKE 14 to 16 minutes on a cookie sheet in oven **OR GRILL** 8 to 10 minutes in covered grill.

Makes 4 servings

Barbecue Sirloin Packet

Prep Time: 10 minutes   ■   **Grill Time:** 20 minutes

1 sheet (18×24 inches)
Reynolds Wrap® Heavy Duty
Aluminum Foil

DRY RUB

2 teaspoons garlic powder

2 teaspoons paprika

2 teaspoons packed brown sugar

2 teaspoons salt

2 teaspoons black pepper

2 teaspoons cayenne pepper

INGREDIENTS

1 pound boneless beef sirloin steak, ½
inch thick, fat trimmed

¼ cup chipotle barbecue sauce

1 medium yellow onion, thinly sliced

1 medium poblano pepper, seeded
and cut into thin strips

PREHEAT grill to medium-high indirect heat. For indirect heat, the heat source (coals or gas burner) is on one side of the grill. Place the food on the opposite side with no coals or flame underneath.

COMBINE ingredients for Dry Rub in a small bowl. Cut steak into thin strips. In a large bowl, combine 2 tablespoons of the rub mixture with the beef strips. Stir in barbecue sauce; set aside. Reserve the remaining Dry Rub for other uses.

CENTER onion slices on sheet of Reynolds Wrap Heavy Duty Aluminum Foil. Top with pepper strips. Arrange beef mixture over onion and pepper in an even layer.

BRING up foil sides. Double fold top and ends to seal, making one large foil packet, leaving room for heat circulation inside.

GRILL 20 to 25 minutes in covered grill over indirect heat.

Makes 4 servings

Reynolds Kitchens Tip

To make your own Chipotle Barbecue Sauce, combine ¼ cup barbecue sauce, 1 tablespoon packed dark brown sugar, 1 tablespoon lime juice and 1 to 2 teaspoons chopped chipotle peppers in adobo sauce.

Index

METRIC CONVERSION CHART

VOLUME MEASUREMENTS (dry)

⅛ teaspoon = 0.5 mL
¼ teaspoon = 1 mL
½ teaspoon = 2 mL
¾ teaspoon = 4 mL
1 teaspoon = 5 mL
1 tablespoon = 15 mL
2 tablespoons = 30 mL
¼ cup = 60 mL
⅓ cup = 75 mL
½ cup = 125 mL
⅔ cup = 150 mL
¾ cup = 175 mL
1 cup = 250 mL
2 cups = 1 pint = 500 mL
3 cups = 750 mL
4 cups = 1 quart = 1 L

VOLUME MEASUREMENTS (fluid)

1 fluid ounce (2 tablespoons) = 30 mL
4 fluid ounces (½ cup) = 125 mL
8 fluid ounces (1 cup) = 250 mL
12 fluid ounces (1½ cups) = 375 mL
16 fluid ounces (2 cups) = 500 mL

WEIGHTS (mass)

½ ounce = 15 g
1 ounce = 30 g
3 ounces = 90 g
4 ounces = 120 g
8 ounces = 225 g
10 ounces = 285 g
12 ounces = 360 g
16 ounces = 1 pound = 450 g

DIMENSIONS

1/16 inch = 2 mm
⅛ inch = 3 mm
¼ inch = 6 mm
½ inch = 1.5 cm
¾ inch = 2 cm
1 inch = 2.5 cm

OVEN TEMPERATURES

250°F = 120°C
275°F = 140°C
300°F = 150°C
325°F = 160°C
350°F = 180°C
375°F = 190°C
400°F = 200°C
425°F = 220°C
450°F = 230°C

BAKING PAN SIZES

Utensil	Size in Inches/Quarts	Metric Volume	Size in Centimeters
Baking or Cake Pan (square or rectangular)	8×8×2	2 L	20×20×5
	9×9×2	2.5 L	23×23×5
	12×8×2	3 L	30×20×5
	13×9×2	3.5 L	33×23×5
Loaf Pan	8×4×3	1.5 L	20×10×7
	9×5×3	2 L	23×13×7
Round Layer Cake Pan	8×1½	1.2 L	20×4
	9×1½	1.5 L	23×4
Pie Plate	8×1¼	750 mL	20×3
	9×1¼	1 L	23×3
Baking Dish or Casserole	1 quart	1 L	—
	1½ quarts	1.5 L	—
	2 quarts	2 L	—